COMMUNITY
RULES

AN EPISCOPAL MANUAL

COMMUNITY RULES

RULES

AN EPISCOPAL MANUAL

IAN S. MARKHAM
AND KATHRYN GLOVER

ILLUSTRATIONS BY BENJAMIN HART

CHURCH
PUBLISHING
INCORPORATED

To Matthew and Lesley
Our soulmates who journey with us.

Church Publishing
19 East 34th Street
New York, NY 10016
www.churchpublishing.org

Cover design by Jennifer Kopec, 2Pug Design
Typeset by Rose Design

A record of this book is available from the Library of Congress.

ISBN-13: 978-1-64065-107-4 (pbk.)
ISBN-13: 978-1-64065-108-1 (ebook)

Printed in the United States of America

Contents

Acknowledgments

We are both grateful to Nancy Bryan, the commissioning editor at Church Publishing who invited us to write this book. Our editor for the book was Milton Brasher-Cunningham. We were impressed with the care with which he read the manuscript and the way he tightened up the text. Thank you, Milton. As colleagues at Virginia Theological Seminary (VTS), we are utterly preoccupied with the question, "What makes Christian community?"

We are also grateful to the following friends and colleagues who graciously read the first draft and provided us with helpful feedback: Matthew Hanisian, Chandler Irvin, Valerie Mayo, KC Robertson, Andrew Rutledge, Alyse Viggiano, Oran Warder, Barbara Warder, and Sophia Weber.

From Ian Markham

I want to express my gratitude to Katie Glover at VTS. As the vice president for Administration and Institutional Effectiveness, she has played a key role in creating a culture that aspires for excellence grounded in Christian values. We have worked together since I arrived, and she has been an extraordinary gift to me. This book is a lovely celebration of our work together.

Katherine Malloy knows how much I enjoy writing; she is very helpful in supporting me in this work. Finally, I am grateful to my wife, Lesley, and my son, Luke, who give me so much joy and so much fun.

From Kathryn Glover

I am grateful to Ian Markham, whose mentorship and encouragement have fostered my ongoing professional growth and development. As dean and president, Ian enables an open environment where exploring new ideas is encouraged and supported even when they do not come to fruition. I am also grateful to the Virginia Theological Seminary staff who show me new ways of understanding and developing our institutional culture. And, finally, to my best friend and husband, Matthew, who asks great questions and cheers me on every step of the way.

From Benjamin Hart

It has been a joy to create illustrations for this lovely book. I am grateful to Ian Markham and Kathryn Glover for allowing me to add my own first interpretation to their writing. I am thankful for the encouragement and the laughter that I regularly share with my colleagues at St. Mathew's here in Louisville. Finally I am grateful for everything I learned about living in a Christian community from my time at Virginia Theological Seminary. Most especially through Amber, Nick, and Jonathan, whose friendship daily brings me joy and makes me a better priest.

Introduction

The Church is a divinely intended community: it is the body of Christ on earth; it is the place where heaven and earth intersect. Yet the reality in our experience can appear otherwise. Church is often hard work. The "politics" of church can be ugly. Sometimes churches are the worst of employers, and sometimes it is difficult to see the connection between Gospel values and the reality of life in a local congregation.

When a congregation fails to live into the values of the Gospel, the damage can be considerable. Life is hard enough during the week. The last thing we need is for Sunday to be hard work, too. When congregations become dysfunctional, it is not surprising that plenty of people decide that the "church of the holy comforter" (i.e., staying in bed) is preferable to church-in-reality.

We need healthy Christian congregations. Our goal with this little book is to distill the theology and practice of church and Christian community into forty-eight simple and clear rules. This book is written for the new member or the seeker and for the confirmation class. It is written for both congregations and Christian organizations. It seeks to weave together Christian beliefs that shape all Christian living with certain applied rules for employment, leadership, and ethos. We have made the congregation the primary organization; for example, there are sections on rules for vestries and rules for parishioners.

But many of the rules would also work for a faith-based organization, or an Episcopal school or seminary.

These are rules for Episcopal community. We are assuming the structure and ethos of the Episcopal Church. However, much of the book would also work for our sister denominations. We hope others in the Christian family will find the book helpful.

Using the Book

The primary venue for this book is a church membership class; the nine sections work nicely for nine sessions where, over a meal, new members can start to understand the nature of Christian community. There are, however, other venues where this book will work well. The vestry can use the book to start discussion around the responsibilities of leadership and Christian community. Alternatively, a rector might want to send one rule a day to a congregation during Lent; after all, it is in Lent that we should be most aware of our obligations to create healthy Christian community that transcends our propensities to sin.

Starting the Journey

We recognize that every community is imperfect. Becoming a Christian community is a process, but it is a process that begins with being intentional. Our prayer is that the result of engaging these rules will be Christian communities that are truly Christian, places where the values of the Gospel are present and evident in our relationships.

Section I

BASIC CHRISTIAN RULES

Christ Is the Foundation
of Christian Community

When **Paul writes to the divided church** at Corinth, he explains that in the end there is just one foundation to all Christian community. He writes, "For no one can lay any foundation other than the one that has been laid; that foundation is Jesus Christ" (1 Corinthians 3:11). Christ is both the inspiration (after all, we are followers of Christ) and the presence (for the resurrected Christ holds Christian community together). When we gather as a Christian community, it is Christ who is in our midst. As Jesus puts it, "For where two or three are gathered in my name, I am there among them" (Matthew 18:20).

Remember That People Are Made in the Image of God

Each person is infinitely valuable. This is fundamental. People are not just complicated bundles of atoms that emerged from nowhere, going nowhere. People are a result of divine love choosing to invite into being the extraordinary gift of each individual. We are all different. Some of us may seem more successful or rich or powerful, but from the divine perspective none of that matters. The gift of life—breathing, thinking, and loving—is the most precious gift of all. Every person is a miracle. Every encounter with a person is remarkable because they embody the gift of life.

3

All People Deserve Respect and Appreciation

We must see people first as beloved children of God and remember they came first into the world as innocent babies. We are called to reach out to them and relate to them as the people they were created to be, and not simply as the people they have become or those our limited vision and understanding allow us to see. We are to recognize the journeys they have been on—even if we don't know what their journeys have been—and take into account the high points, the bumpy roads, and the dark valleys of our own lives as well.

Both Rules 2 and 3 are captured in the baptismal covenant. There, in the concluding declaration, we are all asked: "Will you seek and serve Christ in all persons, loving your neighbor as yourself?" And then, "Will you strive for justice and peace among all people and respect the dignity of every human being?" To these questions, we all reply, "I will, with God's help." It is with God's help that we strive to realize these fundamentals of Christian community.

Welcome, Welcome, Welcome

We have all been there. We have all attended an event, perhaps a party, and not known anyone. We drift toward the bar or the table with the nibbles. We stand, awkwardly perhaps, treating our smartphone as company. Then, before long, we leave, complaining that "It was a very unfriendly place." Meanwhile, those at the event never knew about their mistake; they were too absorbed in catching up with friends, enjoying each other's company. Indeed, when they talk about the event, they commend the place "as a really friendly venue."

Welcome is a conscious activity. It requires looking around the room. It requires noticing who is standing alone. It requires the courage to check in and say, "Hi, I don't think we have met." Welcome is noticing.

A truly welcoming environment is one where we live conscious of those around us; we focus a little less on those who are already friends and focus a little more on those who could become friends.

5

Be Sensitive: We Are All Different

Innocent exchanges can be easily misunderstood. Sometimes they are triggers that remind us of something difficult in our past; sometimes they reveal a distrust of a system; and sometimes we hear something other than what was actually said.

We need to weigh our words with care. We must watch our body language, listen carefully to the response to our words, and ensure that we have been heard as we intended. In the Gospel of Matthew, Jesus is asked by a lawyer which is the greatest of the commandments. Jesus gives a simple reply: " 'You shall love the Lord your God with all your heart, and with all your soul, and with all your mind.' This is the greatest and first commandment. And a second is like it: 'You shall love your neighbor as yourself.' On these two commandments hang all the law and the prophets" (Matthew 22:35–40). Loving our neighbors is fundamental. This must involve being present, understanding, and relating in a deep way. We should love others as we love God and ourselves. When we feel misunderstood, we want others to understand; so, when others feel misunderstood, we must seek to understand.

6

Acknowledge the Other Person's Experience and Perspective

We cannot always agree, but we can honor the lack of agreement and uncover the source. We accept certain differences as natural or fundamental and manage them gracefully. A child cries when they can't have their favorite dessert, so we take time to calm and comfort them. But when an adult gets upset because their idea isn't chosen, we think they should take it in stride.

We form ideas, opinions, and views from our experiences, our knowledge, and our perspectives. There is a part of us in all that we say and do. When we honor a person's presence, words, and actions, we are acknowledging the value of their experience and perspective.

Section II

BASIC CHRISTIAN RULES IN RELATIONSHIP

The first six rules are the fundamentals. They are an intrinsic part of the Christian worldview. In this section, we apply these rules to our relationships with each other. In particular, this is the application of the second rule: remember people are made in the image of God.

7

We Are All Family . . .
Some of Us Are Friends

We don't choose family. Family is a given. Through Christ's death and resurrection to new life, God has made us all brothers and sisters in Christ, which means there is a kinship, an obligation to honor and be there for each other. But like all large families, we are closer to some siblings or relatives than we are to others, perhaps because of shared interests or a shared stage of life. This is not surprising, and it is okay. We honor the entire community of the Church and aspire to recognize the kinship we have in Christ, while we are also allowed to enjoy spending time with particular people.

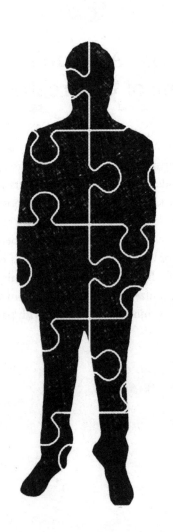

8

Everyone Has a Part to Play in the Body of Christ

Paul, writing to the church in Corinth, offers an inspired image of the Church: it is the "body of Christ" (1 Corinthians 12:12–27). Every part of the body is needed. The foot is as much a part of the body as the hand; and the eye cannot say to the hand that the hand is not needed. Paul's powerful image captures Christian community: everyone is indispensable and valued.

Everyone has a ministry by virtue of our baptism. All roles are important, especially those that are less visible. We are all called by God to find our role and to play that role.

9

Never Be Afraid to Apologize

We all make mistakes—sometimes by design, sometimes inadvertently. Admitting our mistakes through an apology is an acknowledgment of our own humanity and fallibility. It invites others to see and know us more fully, and invites them to be more fully themselves. Being reconciled to each other is a Christian obligation. Jesus says, "So when you are offering your gift at the altar, if you remember that your brother or sister has something against you, leave your gift there before the altar and go; first be reconciled to your brother or sister, and then come and offer your gift" (Matthew 5:23–24). It is never too late to apologize. Sometimes waiting gives the other person time to be readier to hear and accept the apology. Be sincere, straightforward, and clear about the reason for the apology.

10

Learn to Forgive

Just as we are called to apologize to others for our words and actions, we are also called to forgive those who apologize to us. We honor ourselves and the other when we forgive. Both the apology and the act of forgiveness are ways of dealing with the past: they are ways to make sure that true community can be restored. The wrong has been acknowledged, and the wrong has been forgiven. The author of Ephesians explains that we forgive each other because God forgives us in Christ: "Be kind to one another, tenderhearted, forgiving one another, as God in Christ has forgiven you" (Ephesians 4:32).

Confession as part of worship is normally followed with absolution. All of us are invited to confess—lay and clergy alike. The forgiveness that comes through absolution is a gift that God gives to us and that we then share with ourselves and with one another.

Section III

BASIC CHRISTIAN RULES IN COMMUNICATION

In this section, we apply the first six rules to our communication with each other. In particular, this is the application of the third rule: all people deserve respect and appreciation.

11

Be Transparent
in Communication

No one knows what another person is thinking until they speak or write. Words are the way we share our thoughts. Once uttered, words can never be taken back. They enter the realm of the public forever. In the book of James, we are warned that the tongue "is a fire. . . . From the same mouth come blessing and cursing" (James 3:6–10). Therefore, communication needs to be handled very carefully; a reflective silence is often better than a thoughtless word.

We must be clear in all we say and write. We can't hide behind flowery phrases and convoluted sentences. We must think about our message and meaning and strive for clarity and honesty. We are to communicate as much about the joyful and good news as we do about the sad and bad news, and provide both context and reason for our communication, including guidance on how the communication can and should be shared.

12

Think About How
the Communication
Will Be Received

hristian communities will use a variety of different mediums for communication—the Sunday notices, the e-mails, the letters, and the church meetings. The audience for every communication informs not only the message and meaning but also how it will be perceived. To communicate effectively, we must put ourselves in the readers' shoes. What do they need to know? What previous knowledge do they have? Are there any language barriers or cultural differences to take into account? What is their role, and what do we want or need them to do with the information? Will the recipients fail to notice the good news in the midst of our concerns? Or will they miss the bad news hidden in between the meaningless commentary? We must strive to communicate the same message, even if everyone is reading it from their own experience and perspective.

13

Be Considerate—It Is Part of Christian E-mail Etiquette

Let's get really practical. E-mail is a primary means of communication in our modern world. It disappears from our screen, and we trust it arrives quickly. A few seconds, perhaps minutes, lapse. There are a few basics of Christian e-mail etiquette. We must be thoughtful in the construction of the e-mail. We should use a salutation for politeness, and we should be timely in our responses. E-mail must never be written in haste or rage. Sleep on the angry e-mail, and even after run the text past a friend or spouse before sending the message. Civility in our e-mail correspondence is a key part of living in community.

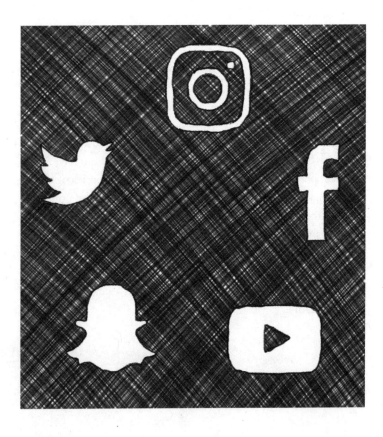

14

Your Social Media Presence Needs to Reflect Grace and Gospel

Social media is a fabulous tool for evangelism and communication, but before we snap, tweet, post, or share, we must remember Rules 1 through 6. Also consider Rule 11. It can be great to post a photo of a recent baptism, but did we first think about our responsibilities to protect children? Is Facebook Live our best tool for sharing that awesome prophetic sermon we preached, or would a single Snap be a better medium? When frustrated by an experience at the DMV and tempted to share it with the rest of the world, remember Rules 1 through 6. And don't forget that others are snapping, tweeting, and sharing about us. Let us be mindful that all we say and do is meant to enhance the body of Christ and to further the coming of God's realm on earth.

Section IV

BASIC CHRISTIAN RULES IN ACTION

In this section, we are bringing together all six of the opening rules. We are made in the image of God; we respect and welcome others; and we relate sensitively to others.

15

Partner With God in Prayer

A dramatic claim of the Christian tradition is that God really wants to hear from us. It is an extraordinary privilege to enter into the presence of God and enjoy the sense of love and support that the Creator of the universe provides. Prayer is never a waste of time. It is the space where we seek to align our will with the will of God to further our service in the world.

We build our relationship with God through prayer. When we participate in corporate prayer, in a congregation, we seek as a community to be focused on what God wants. And it is in our community prayers that we together lift up those who are suffering and in pain. We trust and hope that God's grace will be made manifest in those places of hurt.

16

Give Thanks to God;
Give Thanks to Others

The heart of the Eucharist is the Great Thanksgiving, which is the prayer that the priest says over the bread and wine. Typically, the prayer starts by giving thanks to God for the gift of creation; next it moves to the saving acts of God in history and the message of God's love; and then it culminates in giving thanks for the death of Jesus.

The prayer is an invitation to learn how to be grateful for everything. The alternative to gratitude is indifference or, more seriously, depression and anger. But if we learn the disposition of gratitude, we will start every day grateful for the gift of the moment. And we will look for those things that invite gratitude: the gift of sight, a meal, the love of people around us, good health. We must not presume that these things can be taken for granted. We celebrate with prayers of gratitude to God for the simple things in life.

But there is more. Every human life involves tragedy. Every life suffers illness and finally death. The invitation of the Great Thanksgiving is to learn to see God's grace even in the hard places. As we learn a disposition of gratitude, it flows out. We become people who are grateful for friends and neighbors. Giving thanks is Christianity 101.

Turn Every Worry into a Prayer

There is one part of the Gospel that most Christians think is impossible. Right in the middle of the Sermon on the Mount, Jesus says, "Therefore I tell you, do not worry about your life, what you will eat or what you will drink, or about your body, what you will wear" (Matthew 6:25). The commandment is clear: do not worry.

Worry is strange. It can be consuming. It is often focused on hypotheticals. What if the plane crashes? What if we lose our job? What about our retirement? It is never constructive. It simply spoils the present. Our anxiety stops us from enjoying the moment we are living in.

Jesus tells us to focus on the realm of God. In other words, we are to turn every worry into a prayer and let it go. The test result from the health lab will be what it will be. So give the worry to God. Let God take care of tomorrow. Our task is to be fully present in the moment.

18

Strive for Excellence

Martin Luther, the great Reformer, emphasized a core Christian insight: vocations (that sense of call by God) are not confined to holy orders (being a bishop, priest, or deacon), but can be any profession. God can call a person to be a stockbroker, a nurse, a waitress, or a teacher, or an administrator in an organization. Our vocation does not have to be religious.

This changes everything. If where we are is where God wants us to be, then we are called to do everything as well as we can. To strive for excellence in all we do. To treat our work as a gift to our Creator God who gave us the extraordinary gift of life and the space to live.

19

Don't Hide the Mistakes and the Problems

Jesus alone was sinless. The rest of us are bound to get things wrong from time to time. Sometimes the problems are a result of our egotism, selfishness, and unkindness. Sometimes they are blunders or oversights. Sometimes the problems are not our fault, but we are the ones who have to sort things out.

A Christian community is one that expects mistakes and expects problems. There is the temptation to hide the mistakes and hope the problems will just go away. They do not. The honest and most helpful way forward is to come clean: to identify the mistake and describe the problem. Invite others inside the community to suggest the best way forward. There are always choices. Honesty early on can create better and more attractive alternatives for resolution and forgiveness.

We Are Learning All the Time

Humans are made in the image of God. We are made with the capacity to learn, to reason, and to think. Exercising the capacities of the *Imago Dei* (Latin for "Image of God") is an act of Christian faithfulness. Learning is exciting; learning is life-enhancing; and learning is the exercise of our God-given capacity to reason.

We often imagine that learning stops at the end of school, but this is not right. Every Christian should strive to learn all the time. Attending adult education classes is a good way of learning about our faith. And if we are employed by the Church, then we need to be updating constantly our skill set: learning about new technologies, learning how to do our job in new ways, and learning how to work more effectively as part of the team. These are all important ways of using the *Imago Dei*.

Section V

BASIC CHRISTIAN RULES IN MEETINGS

Meetings are part of the life of all organizations. Church is no exception. From time to time, every member of the congregation will find themselves in a meeting (even if it is just the Annual Meeting of the Church). However, for the vestry, the various committees of the church, and the staff, meetings are a major part of work within the Church. This is the application of Rules 3, 5, and 6; showing respect and appreciation and acknowledging different experiences and perspectives.

Time Is Precious:
Treat Meetings with Respect

Every day is a gift; every moment of every day is a gift. Time is the most precious gift that God gives us.

Meetings, by definition, involve at least two people. On every level, they are expensive. We are using the gift of our time; we are paying for the time of two or more people. The larger the meeting, the harder it is for the meeting to be effective. Therefore, meeting preparation is an important and holy duty.

A good agenda helps. Clarity provided in advance about the meeting's goals is important, and all relevant data should also be collected and shared in advance of the meeting. Some sense of the result of the meeting is also essential. The meeting needs to be chaired well, with everyone included in the conversation. We should strive to make a meeting worthwhile.

22

Bring God into the Meeting Through Prayer, Bible Study, or a Eucharist

Human lives operate on several levels. The "day-to-day" mindset is the normal level where we live, thinking about dinner tonight, worrying about a child, wondering about a job move, or deciding whether an umbrella is needed for the walk to the car. Organizations have an agenda that operates at the "day-to-day" level.

Churches have a massive advantage over other organizations. We are obligated to transform our horizon of thought by bringing the Divine into the very heart of the meeting. This should not just be through the prayer at the beginning, but perhaps by means of a short Bible study, an introduction to a saint, or an analysis of a theological concept. We can move from the "day-to-day" level to the "transcendent" level. Suddenly, the budget discussion is not just how we cut costs, but how we serve the Creator of the universe and advance the realm of God.

23

Have an Agenda: Make Sure Next Steps Are Identified

It is irresponsible for us to gather at a meeting and to feel as though we are convening for a chat. Any meeting, beyond the check-in with a colleague, should have an agenda. Ideally, the agenda is sent out in advance. The work of thinking and data collection that happens before the meeting is very precious. The agenda should have some logic: important items near the top, items that could be tabled nearer the bottom.

The result of the meeting should be clear. The only reason to delay a decision in a meeting is if we need more information. Even with hard decisions, if additional information is not needed, we should stay in the meeting until a decision is made. Delay can be paralyzing for an organization. If everyone is aware of the facts, then press through to the hard decision.

Clarity is also needed as to next steps. Identify the people who will act to write the letter or to organize the event. Identify a date by which the action will be completed. And take minutes to ensure that this happens.

24

Trust the Wisdom of the Group

In any organization, patterns emerge. The extrovert will opine often. The historian will provide background. The naysayer will explain why the idea won't work. The leader will want to have their way. In an undisciplined meeting, the players play their roles. The result is that the collective wisdom of the entire group is not heard.

There are several strategies to overcome such patterns. On contentious topics, go around the table and invite everyone to speak. Break into smaller groups. Introverts are more likely to speak when there are just two or three people in a group. Solicit written contributions.

Once everyone is heard, then a decision needs to be made. Seeking unanimity is often a mistake. It enables a minority to hold an organization hostage. It is good if there is an environment of persuasion, where a case is made and a position emerges that accommodates the concerns of the skeptics. But, sometimes, a vote must be taken. There will be a minority who will be disappointed.

In good organizations, everyone will find themselves on a losing side on some issue at some time. The challenge is to accept the decision, move on, and trust that divine grace will enable the organization to survive and thrive. Continual grumbling is deeply corrosive. Pray for the grace to accept the decision and move on.

Section VI

BASIC CHRISTIAN RULES FOR CLERGY AND EMPLOYEES

A healthy congregation should take an interest in the dynamics among the paid employees of the church. Although this section is focused on the clergy and employees, it is important for the entire congregation to take ownership of these rules. Where necessary, it is helpful when the ethos of the staff is understood and supported by the congregation. This section develops Rules 2, 3, and 5. We recognize we are dealing with the divine in the human, which obligates us to respect and appreciate the other.

25

Honesty Matters: Don't Cheat on Expenses or Time

As Christians, we believe that we are called to excellence in all that we do. In the world of work—whether our employer is secular or not—we must practice what we preach, or at least practice what Jesus preached. We contract with our employers to work a certain number of hours. It is theft when we do not give those hours. In the same way we must not abuse the discretionary fund or take cash from the offering, so we should work hard during our contracted hours.

When things are quiet, we should ask our supervisors how our time could be used effectively. Balance and moderation play a role. If we worked fifty hours last week, working less than forty hours this week may make sense, but it's not all about the numbers as much as the need and result.

It is also important for the congregation to ensure that the clergy and staff are treated fairly. Healthy Christian communities do not exploit those who work for them. Ensuring that there is a season for Sabbath and an appropriate review of salary and benefits are important responsibilities of the congregation. Overall, it is our disposition that matters: we want the church to succeed.

26

Bring Professionalism to the Work with Volunteers

Everyone's time is valuable. That is true for volunteers as well. When a volunteer arrives in the parish office on Friday morning ready to start photocopying the Sunday bulletin, the document should be ready to go. We must provide volunteers with the tools they need to be successful. We must give them a schedule and clear expectations, no matter what their volunteer role may be. Sunday school teacher? Make sure they have a list of the children or young people who are registered for their class. Give them copies of the curriculum well in advance and offer them support in preparing the class. The outreach ministry? Make sure they have access to the building and the inventory to support the ministry. Lay reader? Train them and show them how to access pronunciation guides for all those unfamiliar proper names in Scripture. Be clear about expectations and don't be afraid to hold them accountable. In doing so, they are more apt to take their roles seriously and feel more valued.

27

Feedback Should Be
Frequent and Fair

Nothing is more frustrating than learning that you are not getting your work right. But too many supervisors are nervous about honest feedback. It is a mistake to think that it is kinder to avoid difficult feedback; the result is often a personnel crisis.

Remember to be kind, especially when the feedback may be difficult to hear. When feedback is given frequently, there is less room for surprise. Frequent feedback builds trust and undergirds and clarifies expectations. When we know what is expected of us, we can almost predict what the feedback will be. When the norm for communication is honesty and fairness, we are able to hear feedback with an open and gracious heart. Our personal and professional growth, as well as our development as Christians, is nurtured by feedback that helps us to know and understand ourselves and others more fully.

28

Difficult Tasks and Decisions Won't Go Away

Procrastination rarely brings better results and is rarely an option when others are involved. We need to offer to God, in prayer, the challenges of difficult decisions. The process of decision-making is important. It is essential to have a sense of the priorities in any given situation. We must approach each task and decision with the same mindset: establish a timeframe and time limit that respects everyone involved. We may need to take others into our confidence if we want to explore our options with advisors. We must make sure the advisors are open-minded and do not have a vested interest in the outcome. Ultimately, being willing to press through to a decision is crucial. Putting things off tends to lead to increased anxiety, lost sleep, and added stress. And when we are stressed, we do not make good decisions.

29

Claim Expenses Even When You Don't Want Reimbursement

Parishes and organizations that rely on the financial generosity of others to fulfill their mission need to know how much ministry costs. Resist the temptation simply to pay for the stewardship dinner as part of our financial commitment to the church. The person coming after you may not be able to or want to follow in that tradition. At the very least, you should submit the detail of the expenses. Submitting the receipts and not requesting reimbursement might be considered an in-kind donation and could possibly be claimed as a tax deduction. And what good news it will be for the rector or the treasurer to share the percentage of the operating budget that is funded by in-kind donations.

The Physical and Emotional Well-Being of Employees Matters

hen we consider there are twenty-four hours in a day and a full-time employee spends eight hours working and about an hour on their daily commute (on average), we see that most of us spend at least nine hours every day in work-related activities. We have an obligation to make sure that those are healthy hours for our employees.

How that time is spent and the environment in which the work is done are vitally important. Meeting an employee's physical needs is not merely about providing suitable tools, office furniture, and access to certain facilities. Being mindful of an employee's emotional well-being is more than simply asking them how they are, remembering their birthday, or giving them paid time off. If we cannot afford to contribute to wellness programs like gym memberships or classes, we can have walking meetings, or rent out space for a yoga class and include free employee participation as part of the contract. Observing Rules 1 through 4 will help in establishing and maintaining a happy and positive work environment where employees will enjoy spending time.

31

We Should Be Attentive to the Reasons Why People Move On

Inevitably there are moments when parishioners move on. And there are many good reasons for their doing so. It might be a better opportunity; there might be old friends who are members of the new church. Leaving in these circumstances is good.

It is more concerning when parishioners move on because they are tired of the gossip in the community, or feel that the rector was inattentive to their needs. We should consider and learn from the reasons for their departure.

Even when it successfully follows all the previous rules, a parish may not be the right place for everyone. When there is a mutual decision to part ways, it should be done well and with kindness. And as Rules 9 and 10 remind us, acknowledging our mistakes and wrongdoings through an apology, and accepting that apology from others, are important and vital for healing and moving on. When a member of the community is unhappy, we should seek to understand why and not be afraid to acknowledge any part that we may have played in their unhappiness. Be honest and kind; thank them for being a member of the community and send them off with your prayers for finding a new community where they will be valued and loved.

Make Goodbyes Healthy and Constructive

When it comes to employees, a healthy community should mark their departure. Sometimes the leave-taking is good news, particularly for the one who is leaving: a new opportunity, a call to new ministries, a responsibility to follow a loved one who is changing jobs, or even retirement. Take time to honor the person for all that they have done, and encourage the leave-taker to consider all they have done, all they have learned, and all the ways they have grown. Find tangible examples of their work and highlight them. Don't be afraid to be honest about changes that may come as a result of their leaving. If their position will not be filled or is being made part-time, consider letting them know and helping them to understand why. Finding it out from someone else or through another means might be hurtful and leave them feeling devalued. But resist the temptation of saying, "What will we do without you?" We all know we are not indispensable, and what may seem like a kind word may be received as a meaningless platitude.

33

God's Time . . . Our Time

Remember Rule 25: no matter how many hours we are paid to work, that time should be honored by us and by those with whom and for whom we work. Of course, you will need to take five minutes here or ten minutes there every once in a while to make a doctor's appointment, to text your children to remind them of something, or to take care of other personal matters. But be honest with yourself and with others. If you don't have enough to do, say something. Offer to help a colleague. If you're not getting your work done because you're spending work time doing other things, ask yourself why. Consider talking to someone you trust; maybe there is something to learn from it. If your supervisor or colleague asks you to do something extra, don't just say no. Ask some clarifying questions to understand the request. It might be an opportunity to learn something new and to gain a new sense of satisfaction.

34

Strive to Treat
All Employees Fairly

All employees should have a clear understanding of what is expected of them and what they can expect from others. When employees feel they have been treated unfairly, it is often because they did not have all the information. For example, one employee works a flex schedule; the other doesn't. Inasmuch as it is possible, make decisions based on positions, not people. And when accommodations are made for personal reasons, encourage honesty and transparency. Be clear with others about the parameters and acknowledge and minimize, as much as possible, the effect on others. Show everyone the same level of respect and avoid playing favorites.

Our task is to create an organization that celebrates kingdom values. Everyone matters; everyone is valued; and everyone is, in the words of Rule 2, "made in the image of God."

Section VII

Basic Christian Rules for Vestries

The vestry is the leadership of a congregation. They have a special responsibility for healthy Christian community. They are the bridge between the congregation and the clergy. This section develops all six rules. We are treating people as made in the image of God, and we are striving for a community of welcome, where all are respected.

35

Make a Commitment
and Then Follow Through

Honoring our commitments is always important, but in a volunteer environment it's even more crucial. There may not be someone standing in the wings to pick up where we leave off, so we must think twice before saying yes and make sure we fully understand the commitment we are being asked to make. We then must do all we can to fulfill our promise. We can't be afraid to ask for help if we realize we have taken on more than we can do. Instead of just dumping things in other people's laps, we must offer up what we can do and suggest ideas for how the rest of the commitment might be met. Can someone else be asked to contribute to the task? Would someone in our circle of friends be willing to help, even if they aren't part of our faith community? It might be a means for getting them involved.

36

Listen with an Open Heart
and Open Mind

A **healthy community listens with care.** We must remember the basics of good listening. When a conversation is confidential, it is confidential. We do not gossip. We are discreet when someone shares sensitive and personal information. We also must include all voices.

Lots of organizations are dominated by people who think they know exactly what the next step should be. They are determined to have their vision realized. And they are not interested in anyone else's perspective.

In *The Wisdom of Crowds*, James Surowiecki[1] points out that groups often get things more right than individuals. So simply walking in and deciding something as an individual is not the best for the organization.

We all bring our knowledge, skills, experiences, and perspectives to what we do. Everyone has value and should be honored. In asking others to honor us, we are also sending a message that we honor those with whom we engage and interact. Before disagreeing with someone or disregarding their ideas, let us step back and look at the big picture.

---

1. See James Surowiecki, *The Wisdom of Crowds* (New York: Anchor Books, 2005).

Focus on the Mission and Ministry

Jesus was rarely able to fulfill his ministry without pushback from others. Folks often took offense or found fault with what he was trying to accomplish, where he was trying to accomplish it, and when. But Jesus was so focused on his calling and ministry that he could ignore the heckling and push back against the naysayers.

Most of us do not have to worry about a death sentence for our commitment to mission and ministry, but sometimes our convictions can bump up against resistance and even rejection. As vestry members, our ministry is not only about discerning the will of God but also about telling others about that work and ministry and inviting them to come along. Naturally, we must pray hard to ensure that we are focused on the Gospel mission. Provided that is the case, it is appropriate to trust that God's grace will lead a congregation through the difficult times.

38

Support Your Rector and Clergy

Life for a clergyperson can be hard. They are often present at the hardest times in a parishioner's life—during illness, death, relationship trauma, and loneliness. They are running a volunteer organization, where they are trying to persuade the reluctant to be active. Their operating budget is often small and dependent on pledges. It is difficult to get away; it can be difficult to have an evening to themselves.

A vestry should be sensitive to all this. Both the parish and the vestry need to look out for the rector. We need to respect the "day off" during the week. The Church as a whole, and parishes in particular, are not about the clergy who lead them. Clergy come and go, but the parish community remains. And each clergyperson who passes through has unique gifts and a unique vision to offer. Vestry members, in particular, are not called simply to say yes, but are called instead to ask "Why?" and "How?" in order to discern and act on the will of God for the parish and for God's people—both those within the parish community and those they serve. We must engage the clergy in conversation. Spend time getting to know them and their vision. Ask them questions; tell them when we don't understand or when we disagree. But we can't forget to also tell them, "Well done," when their vision and prayers invite the Holy Spirit into partnership.

39

Hold Your Rector and Clergy to Account

We must scaffold the support and encouragement for the rector and clergy with a healthy dose of critical thinking. Nobody is perfect, and even the most charismatic and thoughtful clergy have their blind spots and weaknesses. If we don't understand a decision or we have concerns about how things are going, we need to make an appointment and talk to the clergy face-to-face. We can't be afraid to tell them we disagree or even that we think they may have made a mistake. But remember Rule 36 and enter the conversation with an open mind and an open heart. They may have a good and valid reason for the decisions they have made. If they have missed the mark, they will be more apt to own it if we approach them in a supportive and open way.

Section VIII

BASIC CHRISTIAN RULES FOR PARISHIONERS

The heart of Christian community is the parish. While earlier sections focused on paid employees of the parish and the volunteer leadership, this section relates to everyone. This section applies Rules 1 through 6 to our role as parishioners and how we relate to and interact with one another.

40

Attend—Not Just Sunday,
but at Least Sunday

Common wisdom says that if we can stick to a new practice for thirty days, it can become a habit. For most of us, church happens once a week on Sundays, so thirty times is about seven months. What would it look like to commit to attending church every Sunday for a year? What would it look like to attend a weekly Bible study, the Wednesday evening class, or weekly services in Lent?

If we are out of town, we can go to church somewhere else. It may seem like the clergy want us to go to church for them—after all, numbers do count—but in the end going to church is more about each of us than it is about the clergy. It's about our relationship with God, and checking in at least once a week is the foundation of that relationship. After a year of weekly attendance on Sundays and during the week, we might just find ourselves missing it in those weeks when we play hooky.

41

Pray on Sunday;
Pray During the Week

Remember Rules 15, 16, and 17 and pray every day. Take time in the service to give thanks, to ask for forgiveness and for strength. Say grace before meals and give thanks to God for the abundance in your life. Pray for the clergy, the vestry, and for others in the parish. Give thanks for their witness and their ministry; ask for guidance and support in resolving differences with others in the parish. Pray especially for those with whom you disagree.

Prayer can happen anywhere. It can be in the car during our commute; it can be as we walk the dog or do our chores. It is good to set some time aside to be still and in the presence of God. The more we pray, the easier it becomes.

Give of Our Treasure

This rule needs to be longer than the others because it is such an important rule. We all know the story of the rich young ruler who asked Jesus, "What must I do to inherit eternal life?" (Mark 10:17). Jesus reminded him of the commandments, and the young man's reply was positive: "Teacher, I have kept all these since my youth." Then Jesus looked and loved the young man and explained, "You lack one thing; go, sell what you own, and give the money to the poor, and you will have treasure in heaven; then come, follow me" (Mark 10:21). It was too much for the young man, and he went away grieving.

The Gospel is clear: our attitude toward possessions—money—is a key aspect of discipleship. The invitation of the Gospel is to see that money often gets in the way of trusting

God. We imagine we need our investment in property, our stocks and shares, as a way of being secure and successful. In truth, the things that really matter—our health, our relationships, our inner well-being—are not determined by material wealth. The quest for material wealth can be very destructive. Plenty of workaholics who are paid well have destroyed their marriages. Material wealth is ephemeral. A stock market crash can significantly erode it. In the end, we all have to learn to trust God. And we should not let our obsession with money obscure the values of the kingdom.

In most parishes, we hear about giving once a year, during stewardship season. But we receive 365 days of the year, so why should giving be a once-a-year kind of thing? Giving is about time, talent, and treasure. (We will discuss giving of our time and talent in Rules 43 and 44.) And we know that where our treasure is, there also is our heart (Matthew 6:21). We tend to give to those things that are meaningful to us. But people, activities, and communities become meaningful to us when we have allowed ourselves the time to become involved and to establish relationships within them. And as easy and tempting as it might be to give of our time and not our treasure, or our treasure and not our talent, we really do need to give of each.

In the end, everything we have is given to us from God. Therefore, we are giving back to God what already belongs to God. This lies behind the rule of the tithe. The old mantra, "Give ten percent, save ten percent, and spend the rest as you like," is a good goal to work toward. We can look at our financial expenses and weigh them against our convictions and commitments. If a morning coffee feels important, how does it weigh against the importance of our membership and participation in a faith community? We might be surprised at how much we actually have to give.

43

Give of Our Time

If you are fortunate and you are blessed to live for 80 years, then you will live for 29,200 days. Life seems to move slowly when young. But before we know where we are, days are flying past. Advent comes around faster and faster each year. Time is a precious gift. Once a moment passes, it is gone forever. The Christian obligation is to ensure that every second is being well used.

Many days disappear in our simple routine. For those who are employed, we wake up, eat breakfast, go to work, come home, watch Netflix, and then go to bed, repeating this process for five days out of seven. The gift of Christian community lifts that time into the eternal. There are many calendars in our lives—a school calendar, a sports calendar, a social calendar—but the most important calendar is the Church year. As we live the Church year, starting with Advent, we are invited to be conscious of the divine narrative as a part of our living. And as we give our time to Christian community, we make those moments eternally significant. Whether it is the altar guild or an outreach ministry, giving of your time to God is the best possible use of this precious gift.

Give of Our Talent

Talent is a combination of inherited skills and training. We all have some talents to share. If we can sing, we can join the choir. If we can organize, we can join an outreach ministry. If we have an aptitude for technology, we can start a social media service for the church. If we are patient and gentle, we can become a Eucharistic minister (a person who delivers the Eucharist to those who are shut in). If we can run, we can do a sponsored run for a charity. If we can see an injustice that needs to be confronted, we can organize a protest.

From the dramatic to the minor, there is a need for our talent. Churches need both people to organize events and people to collect tickets. Some of the most important service is behind the scenes. Learning to serve in whatever capacity we are needed is a deep act of Christian faithfulness.

The other part of time and talent is sharing our gifts and giving our time to one of the parish ministries. Church is not just Sunday worship. Church happens every day of the week. From an outreach ministry that feeds the hungry or clothes the homeless to an internal ministry like the altar guild or the flower guild, we can make a difference.

Getting involved in a midweek ministry adds to our longevity. Sociologists know that church attendance adds two years to a typical human life. If we go to church more than once a week,

we might gain up to seven extra years.[1] It is healthy because we are part of a community, have friends, and find opportunities for learning.

We must make every effort to get involved in two ministries: one might stretch us and even push us outside our comfort zone while offering us an opportunity to deepen our relationship with God and others; the second might be something that has brought us joy and comfort in the past yet still speaks to us and challenges us.

---

1. R. Hummer, R. Rogers, C. Nam, C.G. Ellison, "Religious Involvement and U.S. Adult Mortality," *Demography* 36 (1999): 273–85. This study examined the effect of religious attendance on mortality. People who never attended religious activities exhibited 1.87 times the risk of death compared with people who attended more than once a week. This resulted in a seven-year difference in life expectancy at age twenty between those who never attended and those who attended more than once a week.

45

Go to Coffee Hour

We should get to church in time to center ourselves for worship and should not be tempted to rush out after the dismissal. We can stay and greet the clergy and thank them for their sermon and for the liturgy. We can say hello to someone we don't know. We can go to coffee hour and talk to folks. We can greet the newcomers and make them feel at home. Instead of talking about the weather or our plans for the afternoon, we can talk about what the parish and our faith mean to us and make connections with others on a deeper level. When political topics arise, whether national or church-related, we should graciously listen with an open mind and heart. Be gentle and accepting of the person who says or does something awkward. We can help them to feel more at home and remind them that God does not play favorites.

46

Share Your Faith with Others

The **Great Commission** comes at the end of Matthew. Jesus came and said to them: "All authority in heaven and on earth has been given to me. Go therefore and make disciples of all nations, baptizing them in the name of the Father and of the Son and of the Holy Spirit, and teaching them to obey everything that I have commanded you. And remember, I am with you always, to the end of the age" (Matthew 28:18–20).

We are all called to share the narrative of divine love with others. So many people are lonely, afraid, and fearful, but the Gospel and the Church can be transformative. We have an obligation to share this with others.

This is where we are called to walk the walk and talk the talk. When someone asks us about our weekend, we must not forget to mention church. Simply saying we went to church is a great way to work up to talking about the community, the ministries, and maybe even the sermon or the Christian formation offerings. And as we share, don't be afraid to issue a gentle invitation: "Would you like to come with me one Sunday?"

Section IX

REMEMBER THE BASICS

This book comes full circle. We started with the six basic rules at the beginning, and we conclude with two basic reminders at the end. The Church is a divine entity that should bring joy to ourselves and to the world.

The Church is the Presence of God in a Community

One extraordinary gift that the Gospel gives a human life is that it guarantees both dignity and self-affirmation. The Gospel believes that the Creator of all these planets and galaxies seeks to be in relationship with each individual human being. The Gospel believes that the gathered group on a Sunday morning is the locus of divine action in the world. The Gospel believes that we really matter.

The author of 1 Peter writes, "But you are a chosen race, a royal priesthood, a holy nation, God's own people, in order that you may proclaim the mighty acts of him who called you out of darkness into his marvelous light" (1 Peter 2:9). When we are involved in church work, we are involved in the most awe-inspiring and privileged work in the world. We are right at the nexus of God's connection with this planet. The church is never just an organization; it is indeed the presence of God in the community.

Bring Joy to the Place of Work

We are all projects of God. The Bible talks about God as the potter and all of us as pieces of clay (see Isaiah 64:8). We are being molded by God for the service and challenge of love. Given that our work is the focus of our waking hours, the divine work in our own lives should come radiating out. We should be bringing the presence of Christ into the workplace.

We should start every day with a sense of gratitude. We can take the challenges as moments of learning; take the successes as moments that we give back to God in praise. Bring a smile. Bring a joke. Make the days of those around you a little happier. Learn people's names. Ask after their families. And make sure that the abundance of God's grace in your life bubbles out to those around you.

For Those Who Want to Go Deeper

This is an introductory text. If you want to think further and more deeply about Christian community, then the following books might be helpful.

Barney Hawkins, *Episcopal Etiquette and Ethics: Living the Craft of Priesthood in the Episcopal Church* (New York: Morehouse Publishing, 2010). A delightful meditation on clergy leadership in a congregation. Written with wit and wisdom, it is a profoundly moving text.

Ian S. Markham and Oran E. Warder, *An Introduction to Ministry: A Primer for Renewed Life and Leadership in Mainline Protestant Congregations* (Oxford: Wiley-Blackwell, 2016). Entire chapters on every section described in this book.

John H. Tyson, *Administration in the Small Membership Church* (Nashville, TN: Abingdon, 1996). Small church dynamics are different. This helpful book reflects on those differences.

John W. Wimberly, Jr., *The Business of the Church: The Uncomfortable Truth that Faithful Ministry Requires Effective Management* (Herndon, VA: Alban Institute, 2010). This experienced pastor provides both a theological reflection and many practical tips on the business side of the church.